Prayer & Songbook

Version 1.2

ISBN 978-0-9946018-4-1

www.melanielotfali.com

Prayers   9

- Ala homa 10
- Be as I Am 11
- Blessed is the Spot 12
- Cause of Bounty 13
- Crown of Justice 14
- Educate these Children 15
- Garden of Thy Heart 16
- God Sufficeth 17
- Hollow Reed 18
- Like unto a Pearl 19
- Love Me that I May Love Thee 20
- May You Become as the Waves of One Sea 21
- My Calamity is My providence 22
- O God! Guide Me 23
- O Lord I am Weak 24
- Oh Lord My God, Open Thou the Door 25
- O My Servant! Free Thyself 26
- Patience 27
- Radiant Youth Prayer 28
- Rejoice, Rejoice 29
- Shoreless Oceans 30
- Strive 31
- Thou Art My Lamp 32

Throbbing Artery 33

Where there is Love 34

Whither Shall I Turn 35

Songs 37

Be Like the Earth 39

Bienvenidos 40

Building Bridges 41

Fellowship, Love, Unity 42

Fountain of Generosity 43

God is One 44

He's Got the Whole World 45

His First Counsel 46

Hooray for the World 47

Hoy es el Dia 48

I Think You're Wonderful 49

I Want to be Happy 50

In this Day Bahá'u'lláh 51

Joy Gives Us Wings 52

Lead the Way to Unity 53

Listen 54

Love, Love, Love 56

Look at Me, Follow Me 58

Looking for Good 60

Magic Penny	62
Months of the Year	63
Mount your Steeds	64
One Planet, One People	65
One Heart, Ruby Red	66
Prince of Peace	68
Queen of Carmel	69
See Me Beautiful	70
Shine Your Light on Me Bahá'u'lláh	71
Singing Wind	72
Tell the Truth	73
Teaching Peace	74
That is How Bahá'is Should Be	75
This Little Light of Mine	76
Toko Zani	77
Truthfulness	78
We are Drops	79
We have Come to Sing Praises	80
With Two Wings	81
Would You Give Your Life to Bahá'u'lláh	82

The art of music must be brought to the highest stage of development, for this is one of the most wonderful arts and in this glorious age of the Lord of Unity it is highly essential to gain its mastery. However, one must endeavour to attain the degree of artistic perfection and not be like those who leave matters unfinished. - Abdu'l-Bahá

O nightingale of the rose-garden of God! Singing melodies will bring animation and happiness to the world of humanity, the hearers will be delighted and joyful and their deeper emotions stirred. But this gladness, this sense of emotion is transitory and will be forgotten within a short time. However, praise be to God, thou hast blended thy tunes with the melodies of the Kingdom, wilt impart solace to the world of the spirit and wilt everlastingly stimulate spiritual feelings. This will last forever and endure the revolution of ages and centuries.

O servant of Bahá! Music is regarded as a praiseworthy science at the Threshold of the Almighty, so that thou mayest chant verses at large gatherings and congregations in a most wondrous melody and raise such hymns of praise at the Mashriqu'l-Adhkar to enrapture the Concourse on High. By virtue of this, consider how much the art of music is admired and praised. Try, if thou canst, to use spiritual melodies, songs and tunes, and to bring the earthly music into harmony with the celestial melody. Then thou wilt notice what a great influence music hath and what heavenly joy and life it conferreth. Strike up such a melody and tune as to cause the nightingales of divine mysteries to be filled with joy and ecstasy.

Prayers

Ala homa

Al-laa-home-ma, Yaa Sobe-Boo-Hone, Yaa Ghoed-doos
(O my God lauded art Thou, O Thou to Whom praise is due,
O Thou the sanctified One)

Ya Han-nunoe Yaa Man-nun
(O Thou the Sanctified One, O Thou the Hallowed One)

Al-laa-home-ma, Yaa Sobe-Boo-Hone, Yaa Ghoed-doos
(O my God lauded art Thou, O Thou to Whom praise is due,
O Thou the sanctified One)

Ya Han-nunoe Yaa Man-nun
(O Thou the Sanctified One, O Thou the Hallowed One)

Far-re-ge La-naa Bel Faz-leh Val Eh-sun
(Remove our difficulties through Thy Bounty & Beneficence)

En-na-ka Rah-maa Noen Man-nun
(Thou verily art the Merciful & Hallowed)

En-na-ka Rah-maa Noen Man-nun
(Thou verily art the Merciful & Hallowed)

Baha'u'llah, Baha'u'llah, Baha'u'llah

Baha'u'llah, Baha'u'llah, Baha'u'llah

Be as I Am

Look at me, follow me
be as I am
'Abdu'l-Baha, 'Abdu'l-Baha

(repeat)

Blessed is the Spot

```
   A              Amaj7
Blessed is the spot
         A7          D
and the house and the place
        Dm           Dm
and the city and the heart
       A         A
and the mountain


         A             Amaj7
And the refuge and the cave
         A7          D
and the valley and the land
        Dm           Dm
and the sea and the island
       A         A
and the meadow


 E7              E7
where mention of God
         A       A
hath been made
         E7   E7        A  Amaj7  A7  D
and His praise,    glori-fied
 Dm    Dm        A
Ooooh, ooooh, Bahá'u'lláh
```

Cause of Bounty

Make me a cause of bounty
to the human world
and crown my head
with the diadem
of eternal life
'Abdu'l-Baha

Crown of Justice
-Bahá'u'lláh, Epistle to the Son of the Wolf, p. 12-13

Say: O God, my God!
Attire mine head
with the crown of justice
and my temple with the ornament
of equity
Thou, verily
art the Possessor
of all gifts and bounties

Educate these Children

'Abdu'l-Baha, Baha'i Prayers, p. 35-36

```
D  A    G              A
O God! Educate these children

D       A              G       A
These children are the plants of Thine orchard

        G            D
The flowers of Thy meadow

      G           D
the roses of Thy garden

           G          D
Let Thy rain fall upon them

         G       D                        A
Let the Sun of Reality shine upon them with Thy love

            D
Let Thy breeze refresh them

     G                A       D
in order that they may be trained

    G       D          G             A
Grow and develop, and appear in the utmost beauty

D   G     D        G  D
Thou art the Giver

              G  A    D
Thou are the Compassionate!
```

Garden of Thy Heart

In the garden of thy heart
plant naught but the rose of love
Bahá'u'lláh

(repeat)

God Sufficeth

Unknown Origin

```
         D
Say God sufficeth
G           A
all things above all things
       D              G
and nothing in the heavens
        A
or the earth
       D      G  A
but God sufficeth

   D     G            A
Verily He is in Himself
        D
the Knower
       D
Sustainer
       G  A   D
the Omnipotent
```

Hollow Reed
by George Townsend

```
    Am      F           Em      Am
O God!   Make me a hollow reed
                    F         Em              Am
From which the pith of self hath been blown
          C      D           F7    E7
So that I may become a pure channel
E7                    F         E7      Am
   Through which Thy love may flow unto others
```

Like unto a Pearl

```
He is God! (echo)
O God, my God! (echo)
Bestow upon me a pure heart (echo)
Like unto a pearl (echo)
```

Love Me that I May Love Thee

```
 C                 F
Love Me that I may love thee
 G         C
If thou lovest Me not
 C                     F
My love can in no wise reach thee
   G         C
Know this O servant
```

May You Become as the Waves of One Sea

'Abdu'l-Baha, The Promulgation of Universal Peace, p. 213-215
Music by Joe Crone - *Immerse Yourselves*, CD

```
 C         F           G            C     F  G
May you become as the waves of one sea
  C   F G      C    F  G
Stars of the same heaven
C       F G           C   F  G
 Fruits adorning the same tree
C   F  G  C    F  G
 Roses of one garden
F              G
 In order that through you
         C       Am
The oneness of humanity
 F
May establish its temple
G            C     F  G  ... C
In the world of mankind
```

(repeat)

My Calamity is My providence

Words by Baha'u'llah, Hidden Words of Baha'u'llah, part I. #51, p. 15
Music by Rob Allan

```
C        G   F         C
My calamity is My providence

C           G     F         C
Outwardly it is fire and vengeance

        C      G     F        C
but inwardly it is light and mercy

 F      G  C
Hasten thereunto


    C        G      F
That thou mayest become

F   G    C      C       G       C
an eternal light and an immortal spirit

   C          G      F
This is My command unto thee

 F    G    C
do thou observe it
```

O God! Guide Me

O God!
Guide me
Protect me
Make of me

A shining lamp
and a brilliant star
Thou art the Mighty and
the Powerful

MAORI
E te Atua
E te Atua
Arahina I ahau
Tiakina ahau
Whakamaramatia
Te rama o toku manawa

Kia meinga ahau
Hei whetu tiahoaho
Ko koe
Ko koe te kaha rawa
Me te Mana

O Lord I am Weak

O Lord
I am weak   (together)
Strengthen me   (together)
With Thou power and Thy potency   (together)

My tongue falters   (echo)
Suffer me to utter   (echo)
Thy commemoration and praise   (together)

I am lowly   (echo)
Honor me   (echo)
Through admitting   (echo)
Me into Thy kingdom   (echo)
Me into Thy kingdom

(repeat)

Oh Lord My God, Open Thou the Door

O Lord my God   (echo)
Open Thou the door   (echo)
Prepare the means   (echo)
Make safe the path and guide the way   (everyone)

For verily Thou art   (echo)
The Help in Peril   (echo)
The Self-Subsisting   (echo)
Ya Baha'u'l-Abha   (echo)

O My Servant! Free Thyself

Adapted from Hidden words of Baha'u'llah, part II. #40, #39, #41, p. 36
Music by Ravi Shankar. Choral Arrangement by Tom Price
From "On Wings of the Soul", 3rd Edition, 1994
Compiled and edited by Elaine Merrill Losey, Baha'i National Center, Seoul, Korea

Free thyself from the fetters of this world
Loose thy soul from the prison of self
Seize thy chance. Seize thy chance
O......... My Servant!

Didst thou behold a sovereignty immortal
Thou wouldst strive to pass from this world
Fleeting world. Fleeting world
O......... My Servant!

Ah............
Be not content with the ease of a passing day
Be not deprived of everlasting rest
Trade not the garden of eternal delight
For the dustheap of a mortal world

Up from thy prison ascend unto glory
Up from thy prison ascend unto glory
And from thy mortal cage wing thy flight
O......... My Servant

Patience

Unknown origin. Capo 2nd fret.

VERSE 1

```
      A                        A/B
The steed of this Valley is patience
       D                  A
Without patience the wayfarer
A                       A/B
On this journey will reach nowhere
      D              A
And attain no goal... no goal
```

```
E                    D
 Nor should he ever be downhearted
E                    D
 If he strive for a hundred thousand years and yet fail
E            D                       D
 To behold the beauty of the Friend, the beauty of the
Friend
```

```
A             A/B     D
 He should not falter (should not falter)   (x2)
```

```
A             A/B
 He should not falter
     D                E           D             E
A hundred thousand years, the beauty of the Friend
```

(repeat verse 1)

Radiant Youth Prayer

'Abdu'l-Baha - Baha'i Prayers 2009, p.254
Capo - 8th fret - C, G, Em, D, Am

O Lord! Make this youth radiant
And confer Thy bounty upon this poor creature

Bestow upon him knowledge, grant him added strength
At the break of every morn

And guard, him, within, the shelter of Thy protection
So that he, may, be freed from error

May devote himself to the service, of Thy Cause

(May) Guide the wayward, lead the hapless
Free the captives, awaken the heedless
x4

That all may be blessed with Thy remembrance and praise
x4

Thou art the Mighty and the Powerful
That all may be blessed with Thy remembrance and praise
x2

That all may be blessed with Thy remembrance and praise
x2

Rejoice, Rejoice

Unknown origin. Capo 1st fret.

VERSE

```
Bm          D          A
   Thus I exhort each of you
      G              D#/F
To sacrifice all your
Bm          D          A
   Thoughts words and actions
      G              D#/F          Bm
To bring the knowledge of the love of God
      D                A
Into every heart, into every heart
      G              D#/F
Knowledge of the love of God
```

(repeat)

```
D     A            G
   Ye must in this matter
D      A                G
   That is the serving of humankind
D      A          G
   Lay down your very lives
      G                                    Bm
And as ye yield yourselves rejoice, rejoice
      D              G                    Bm
And as ye yield yourselves rejoice, rejoice
      D              G                    Bm
And as ye yield yourselves rejoice, rejoice
      D              G                    Bm-A
And as ye yield yourselves rejoice, rejoi-oice
```

(4 bar interlude)

(Verse x2 - End on Bm)

Shoreless Oceans

PART 1

```
   G            C
Were ye to discover, the hidden, the shoreless oceans   (x2)

G           C
of My incorruptible wealth
G           C         D
of My incorruptible wealth
```

PART 2

```
   G       C
ye would, of a certainty, esteem as nothing, the world  (x2)


   G       C
nay, the entire creation (together)
```

Strive

Words from 'Abdu'l-Bahá, Paris Talks, p. 81
Music by Joe Crone - *Immerse Yourselves*, CD

```
    G              Am7          D        G
Strive that your actions day by day may be
            Am7        D
beautiful prayers

    G              Am7            D
Turn towards God and seek always to do
                    G        D
that which is right and noble
```

```
Am7  D       G
 Enrich the poor
Am7  D       G
 Raise the fallen
Am7  D       G
 Comfort the sorrowful
         Am7
Bring healing to the sick
D
Reassure the fearful
  Am7
Rescue the oppressed
        D
bring hope to the hopeless
  Am7           D
Shelter the destitute!
```

(repeat all)

```
    G   Am7   D
Strive            (x5)
```

Thou Art My Lamp
The Hidden Words of Bahá'u'lláh

Thou art My lamp
and My light is in thee
Get thou from it thy radiance
and seek none other than Me
For I have created thee rich
and have bountifully shed My favor upon thee

Throbbing Artery

Unknown Origin

```
       Am          Dm         Am
Be thou as a throbbing artery
       Am      Dm       Am
Pulsating in the body
              G      Am    G    Am
Of the entire creation
```

```
          Am         Dm        Am
That through the heat generated
G        Am          G     Am
By this motion there may appear
```

```
      Am         Dm         Am
That which will quicken the hearts
       G      Am      G   Am
Of those who hesitate
```

Where there is Love

Arrangement by Skye Lotfali & NCCI friends
Verse 1 & verse 2 can be sung at the same time

VERSE 1

```
                C
Where there is love
                G
Where there is love
  Am
Nothing is too much trouble
  F7
Nothing is too much trouble
```

(Verse 1)

VERSE 2

```
                  C
There's always time, time, time, time, time
                  G
There's always time, time, time, time, time
                  Am
There's always time, time, time, time, time
  F7
There's always time
```

(repeat all)

(Verse 1)

34 - Prayers

Whither Shall I Turn

Unknown origin. Capo 2nd fret.

VERSE 1

```
   Am                              C
Wither shall I turn, wither shall I turn
          G                D
powerless as I am to discover
Am                    C
Any other way, any other way except
            G           D
the way that Thou didst set
```

(repeat)

```
        Am            C
All the atoms of the earth
            G             D
proclaim Thee to be God and testify
        Am              C
that there is none other God
            G         D
besides Thee, besides Thee
```

```
    Am      C         G          D
So whither, whither shall I turn, O my God   (x2)
              Am       C                G       D
Powerless as I am, I am, powerless as I am, I am   (x2)
```

(repeat all)

(repeat verse 1)

Prayers - 35

36 - Prayers

Songs

Be Like the Earth
Ruhi Institute

```
  C       G      F      G    C
See the earth, It's so humble
        C                 G
Has all God's wealth to give
 F            G       C
Everything we need to live
            C                G
Lets us walk on it every day
                F       G      C
But have you ever heard it say
  C    G       F  G         C
"I am richer, Greater than you"


  C       G     F    G  C
See the tree, It's so humble
       C               G
The more its fruits abound
 F              G        C
It bows closer to the ground
         C                   G
And shares the fruit that way
                F       G      C
But have you ever heard it say
  C    G       F  G         C
"I am richer, Greater than you"


  C            G
Be like the earth
 F G         C
Be like the tree
  C                       G
Rise to the heaven of glory
        F              G   C
On the wings of humility
  C                       G
Rise to the heaven of glory
        F              G   C
On the wings of humility
```

Bienvenidos
"Welcome" - Unknown Origin

```
 F              C              Em           Am
Bienvenidos hermanos, a la Fe Baha'i
 F              C              Em           Am
Bienvenidos hermanos, a la Fe Baha'i
```

CHORUS
```
  F             C            Em           Am
En este momento, estamos contentos
 F              C               Em                  Am
Bienvenidos, Allah'u'Abha, Bienvenidos, Allah'u'Abha
   Am           F            C          Em       Am
Allah'u'Abha, Allah'u'Abha, Allah'u'abha
```

Bienvenidos hermanos al hogar del amor
Bienvenidos hermanos al hogar del amor

(Chorus)

Bienvenidos hermanos sean muy felices
Bienvenidos hermanos sean muy felices

(Chorus)

Building Bridges
by Jackie Elliot

CHORUS

                G
We're building bridges out of the walls

         D
Building bridges out of the walls

         D   A
Building bridges out of the walls

          D
That keep us apart

     D   A
When the wall says stay away, we're from a different land
A   D
Gonna tell them, the earth's one country and we're world citizens
             D   G
And turn that wall into a bridge. Take my brother by the hand
            D   A   D
And walk across that bridge to the world God promised man

(Chorus)

     D   A
When the wall says stay away, we're from a different race
A
We're going to tell them there's just one race
               D
   and that's the human race
            D   G
And turn that wall into a bridge. Take my sister by the hand
            D   A   D
And walk across that bridge to the world God promised man

(Chorus)

     D   A
When the wall says stay away, our religions aren't the same
A   D
We're going to tell them we just worship God by different names
            D   G
And turn that wall into a bridge. Take my family by the hand
            D   A   D
And walk across that bridge to the world God promised man

(Chorus x2)

Fellowship, Love, Unity
Unknown Origin

```
 C                  F
Long time ago in Mazindiran
 G                  C
So the Dawnbreakers say
 C                      F
A Manifestation of God was born
     G                    C
Bringing the Promised Day - and He sang
```

CHORUS
```
  C                          F
Fellowship, fellowship, love, love, unity
 G                C
All the people are one
 C                         F
Man is a member of just one family
         G              C
The Age of Peace has begun
```

Mulla Husayn came down to Shiraz
And found the Point of Bayan
Say, Mulla Husayn go tell all the people
The Prophet He speaks again - and He sang - **(Chorus)**

Now the Shah thought he could put out the Light
By putting our Lord from Iran
Say, Shah what a foolish man you are
The Teachings have only begun - and they say - **(Chorus)**

Now Abdu'l-Baha says always be happy
Laughing and singing and so
I want you should all join in the refrain,
By now you should know how it goes - and we say - **(Chorus x2)**

```
         G              C
The Age of Peace has begun
The Age of Peace has begun
```

Fountain of Generosity
by Mildred N. McClellan

       C
Be a fountain, be a spring
   C   **G**
Be an ever-flowing thing
      F   **C**
It is true that if you do
Dm7   **G7**   **C**
Happiness will come to you
              F   **C**
Search your heart every day
        D7   **G7**
Is there something you can give away

    C
Happiness should be your goal
       C   **G**
Give your heart, and give your soul
     F   **C**
It is true that if you do
Dm7   **G7**   **C**
God will always be with you
           F   **C**
Search your heart every day
      D7   **G7**
Is there something you can give away

    C
Happiness should be your goal
       C   **G**
Give your heart, and give your soul
     F   **C**
It is true that if you do
Dm7   **G7**   **C**
God will always be with you

God is One

Lift up Your Voice, Vol. 1, CD

```
   C            G
God is One; man is one
      C
And all the religions are one
 G              C
Land and sea, hill and valley
 D                G
Under the beautiful sun
```

CHORUS
```
   C            G
God is One;  man is one
      C                   C7
And all the religions agree
            F                      C
When everyone learns the three onenesses
            G        C
We'll have world unity
```

```
   C           G
God is love. God is light.
      C
And all are as one in His sight
 G              C
Black and white, red and yellow,
  D                G
this is the time to unite
```

(Chorus)

He's Got the Whole World
Traditional spiritual

              D
He's got the whole world in his hands
              A
He's got the whole wide world in his hands
              D
He's got the whole world in his hands
              D   **A**   **D**
He's got the whole world in his hands

He's got you and me and brother in his hands
He's got you and me and sister in his hands
He's got you and me and brother in his hands
He's got the whole world in his hands

He's got the mommas and the papas in his hands
He's got the grandmas and the grandpas in his hands
He's got the uncles and the aunts in his hands
He's got the whole world in his hands

He's got the little bitty baby in his hands
He's got the little bitty baby in his hands
He's got the little bitty baby in his hands
He's got the whole world in his hands

He's got the whole world in his hands
He's got the whole wide world in his hands
He's got the whole world in his hands
He's got the whole world in his hands

His First Counsel

By Wiley Rinaldi

```
 A
Listen to the voice
         A
That makes our hearts rejoice
      G         D        A
His first counsel is this
 E
Possess a pure heart
    A
A kindly heart
   B7        E
A radiant heart


         D        A
The heart is a treasure
    D        A
A gift beyond measure
    B7           E
A bounty from your Lord
      D            A
Protect it from the fire
    D       A
Of worldly desire
        D   E    A
And freely let it soar
```

Hooray for the World

Music & Lyrics by Red and Kathy Grammer, *Teaching Peace*, CD

CHORUS

    C   G
Hooray for the world, I'm glad to be on it
    G   C
Hooray for the world, I'm glad to be on it
    C   F
Hooray for the world, it's a special place
            G   C
We've got mother nature and the human race

    C   F
The world's got buffalo, the world's got bees
    C   F   G
The world's got jellyfish swimming in the seas
      C   F
We've got beavers and bears, bats and bugs
 G
Miniature poodles and slimy old slugs

(Chorus)

    C   F
The world's got salami, the world's got cheese
      C   F   G
We've got maple syrup and mulberries
      C   F
We've got Egg Foo-Yung, bagels and lox
 G
Corn on the cob, and raisins in a box, so

(Chorus)

      C   F
We've got moms and dads, uncles and aunts
    C   F   G
Brothers, sisters, grandmas and gramps
      C   F
We've got neighbors next door, kids down the street
 G
Everywhere we go we've got new friends to meet, oh

Hoy es el Dia

Unknown Origin

```
  Am                      Dm
Hoy es el dia de la Puerta de la Gloria
  Am                E     Am
Hoy es el dia de Ali el Bab
  Am                      Dm
Hoy es el dia de la Puerta de la Gloria
  Am                E     Am
Hoy es el dia de Ali el Bab

  Dm              Am
Hoy es el dia, Hoy es el dia
  E                     Am
Hoy es el dia de Ali el Bab
  Dm              Am
Hoy es el dia, Hoy es el dia
  Em     Am
Hoy - ya!
```

Hoy es el dia de la Gloria de Dios
Hoy es el dia de Baha'u'llah

Hoy es el dia del Siervo de la Gloria
Hoy es el dia de Abdu'l-Baha

Hoy es el dia de la Unidad del Mundo
Hoy es el dia de la Fe Baha'i

Hoy es el dia de amor y amistad
Hoy es el dia de la paz munidal

I Think You're Wonderful

Music & Lyrics by Red and Kathy Grammer, *Teaching Peace*, CD

CHORUS

```
C                                                  G
I think you're wonderful, when somebody says that to me
G                             C
I feel wonderful, as wonderful can be
C                                                F
It makes me want to say the same thing to somebody new
F                         C
And by the way I've been meaning to say
G                       C
I think you're wonderful too
```

```
    C                                       G
When we practice this phrase in the most honest way
   G                       C
Find something special in someone each day
   C                 F
Lift up the world one heart at a time
G                            G7
It all starts by saying this one simple line
```

(Chorus)

```
    C                                     G
When each one of us feels important inside
   G                      C
Loving and giving and glad we're alive
C                            F
Oh, what a difference we'll make in each day
G                                 G7
All because someone decided to say
```

(Chorus)

I Want to be Happy

Unknown Origin

   Am
There is something you must know
                          E7
In this Faith we have to show
Dm
We are men of deeds, not of words
     Am   **E7**   **Am**
Our very life should show our Faith to friend and foe

CHORUS

    Am   **Am**
I want to be happy, I want to be strong
    Am   **Am**
To be His servant, my whole life long
      Dm   **Am**
So, I must obey the laws of God
     E7   **Am**
Yes, I must obey the laws of God

   Am
There is something you must know
                          E7
In this world of pomp and show
Dm
People are tired of empty speech
      Am   **E7**   **Am**
They want to see you practice what you teach

(Chorus)

In this Day Bahá'u'lláh

by Frederick Ward, *We have come to Sing Praises*, CD

```
  A            D
In this day Baha'u'llah
  A                         E
Talking to the world about justice
  A                D
Oh what a wonder this justice
  A          E       A
Surely it's the day of God


  A            D
In this day Baha'u'llah
  A                         E
Talking to the world about oneness
  A                D
Oh what a wonder this oneness
  A          E       A
Surely it's the day of God


  A              E        A
Blessed Beauty. Blessed Beauty
D          A    E-A-D-E
Alleluia, He is come


  A            D
In this day Baha'u'llah
  A                         E
Talking to the world about oneness
  A                D
Oh what a wonder this oneness
  A          E       A
Surely it's the day of God
```

Joy Gives Us Wings
by Joan Lincoln

```
  D   A       D       G   G   A       D
Joy gives us wings to fly, joy gives us wings
Joy gives us wings to fly, joy gives us wings
          A             D
In times of joy, our strength grows in might
In times of joy, our intellect takes flight
In times of joy, our understanding is bright
  D   A       D       G   G   A       D
Joy gives us wings to fly, joy gives us wings
```

```
  Dm              A7          Dm       A7     Dm
But when sadness visits us, when sadness visits us
   A                     Dm
We become weak, our strength goes away
   A                       Dm
Our insights are dim, our thoughts become gray
  A7
How-ev-er...
```

```
  D   A       D       G   G   A       D
Joy gives us wings to fly, joy gives us wings
Joy gives us wings to fly, joy gives us wings
          A             D
In times of joy, our strength grows in might
In times of joy, our intellect takes flight
In times of joy, our understanding is bright
```

```
  D   A       D    G
Joy gives us wings to fly
  G    A       D
Joy... Gives... Us wings
```

Lead the Way to Unity
Unknown Origin

CHORUS

D
We lead the way to unity
G
we lead the way to unity
D
we lead the way to unity
A
we lead the way

Voice #2
We all know that peace is on the way

```
 D                       G
Hush my brother, don't cry my brother a
 D          A
new day has begun
 D                       G
Smile my sister, sing out my sister
 D          A
the world will soon be one
```

(Chorus)

```
D                    G
In the village, in every village
    D                A
The seed of love we'll sow
```

```
D                    G
In the nation, in every nation
    D                A
a tree of faith will grow
```

(Chorus)

Listen

Music & Lyrics by Red and Kathy Grammer, *Teaching Peace*, CD

```
  G              G
Listen - can you hear the sound
  G         C          G
Hearts beating, all the world around
  C     D      C            G
Down in the valley, out on the plains
  C         D                C              G
Everywhere around the world, the heartbeat sounds the same
```

CHORUS
```
  C          D        G
 Black or white, red or tan, it's the
                         C
heart (sound, song) of the family of man
 G   D                                   C
 Whooo, beating (laughing, singing) away
     D                                   C
 Whooo, beating (laughing, singing) away
     D                               G
Whooo, beating (laughing, singing) away
```


```
  G              G
Listen - can you hear the sound
  G      C           G
Laughter - all the world around
  C      D       C          G
High in the mountains, down by the sea
  C         D                C            G
Everywhere around the world, laughter sounds the same to me
```
(Chorus)

```
C                              D
Ooo-ooo la la la la la, Ooo-ooo la la la la la
C                               D                  G        D
Ooo-ooo la la la la al, Ooo-ooo la la la la la, La-ah-ah, Oh
```
(repeat)

```
  G              G
Listen - Can you hear the sound
  G      C          G
```

54 - Songs

Singing - all the world around
```
 C              D        C              G
```
Walkin' through the jungle, or on a busy city street
```
C            D              C                    G
```
Everywhere around the world, singing always sounds so sweet

(Chorus)

Love, Love, Love

by Creadell Haley

```
    C          F        G                C
Love, love, love, love, love your fellow man
    C          F        D7              G
Love, love, love is how the world began
    C          F         C         G
God loved creation, so He created thee to
    C          F        G           C
Love, love, love Him and humanity


    C          F        G              C
Love, love, love the ever-lasting good
    C          F        D7              G
Love, love, love the seed of brotherhood
    C          F         C      G
Love all creation, for He created thee to
    C          F        G           C
Love, love, love Him and humanity


    C          F        G               C
Love God's creatures be they near or far
    C          F        D7              G
See each human, as a shining star
    C          F         C      G
Love all creation, for He created thee to
    C          F        G           C
Love, love, love Him and humanity
```

Look at Me, Follow Me

Words and music by Jackie Elliot & Tom Price. *Lift up your Voices*, Vol. 1, CD
Based on statements of 'Abdu'l-Bahá

```
 D          A            G              D
 Behold a candle, how it gives its light
Bm                                Em              A
 It weeps its life away drop by drop to give its flame
 D              A          G           D
You must die to the world, and so be born again
 Bm                        Em  A
And enter the Kingdom of Heaven
```

CHORUS
```
          D        G       D   D
Look at Me, follow Me, be as I am
         Em    A       D
'Abdu'l-Bahá, 'Abdu'l-Bahá
```

```
 D          A         G              D
 You are the angels, if your feet be firm
Bm                           Em              A
 Be steadfast as a rock that no earthly storm can move
 D         A      G                D
And as you have faith so shall your powers be
 Bm                          Em      A
And know that 'til the end I'm always with you
```

```
          D        G       D
Look at Me, follow Me, be as I am
         Em    A       D
'Abdu'l-Bahá, 'Abdu'l-Bahá
          D         G       D
Love Mankind, follow Me, be as I am
         Em    A       D
'Abdu'l-Bahá, 'Abdu'l-Bahá
```

```
D                         A                    G              Bm
And how I long to travel the world in utmost poverty
                     D           G                  A
And cry out Ya Baha! God willing you may do this for Me


              D              G     D
Teach the Cause, follow Me, be as I am
       Em      A       D
'Abdu'l-Bahá, 'Abdu'l-Bahá
        D              G     D
Serve Mankind, follow Me, be as I am
       Em      A       D
'Abdu'l-Bahá, 'Abdu'l-Bahá
     D                G    D
Look at Me, follow Me, be as I am
       Em      A       D
'Abdu'l-Bahá, 'Abdu'l-Bahá
```

Looking for Good
by David Hunt

   C
I've got excellence as my goal
         F7
But I've got a long, long way to go
       C
And I know it helps me on my way
       G7
When I see the good in every day
       F7
So if I see something you do wrong
  C
I won't sing about it in this song
  G7
I won't talk about it with my friends
  F7
I won't even think about it again

CHORUS
    F7
I'll look at the good in you
    C
I'll look at the good in you
   G7
I know that you'd want me to
      F7
'Cause that's what I'd want you to do
    F7
And God looks for the good in me
  C
He looks for the good in me
   G7
And when I put a cover
    F7
On those little faults of others
     C   **G7**   **C**
I hope God will put a cover on my faults too

    C
'Abdu'l-Bahá was very wise
    F7
He saw your heart inside your eyes
      C
And when He noticed something wrong
    G7
He'd find some way to make you strong
   F7
So if I find some fault in you
  C
I know just what I have to do
   G7
I won't go tell anybody else
    F7
No, I won't even tell myself

(Chorus)

Magic Penny
Unknown Origin

```
 C
Love is something if you give it away
 G           C
give it away, give it away
 C
Love is something if you give it away
      G              C
it comes right back to you
```

CHORUS
```
 F              C
It's just like a magic penny
 G                      C
hold it tight and you won't have any
 F              C
Lend it, spend it, give it away
      G              C
it comes right back to you
```

```
 C
A smile is something if you give it away
 G           C
give it away, give it away
 C
A smile is something if you give it away
      G              C
it comes right back to you - (chorus)
```

```
 C
A hug is something if you give it away
 G           C
give it away, give it away
 C
A hug is something if you give it away
      G              C
it comes right back to you - (Chorus)
```

Months of the Year
Unknown Origin

```
  C         G         C
Bahá, Jalál, Jamál
  C         G       C
'Azamat, Núr, Rahmat
  F           C       G   C
Kalimát, Kamál, Asmá
  C         G              C
'Izzat, Mashíyyat, 'Ilm
  F
Qudrat, Qawl, Masá'il, Sharaf
  C        G       C
Sultán, Mulk, 'Alá
```

```
     C          G            C
Splendor, Glory, and Beauty
    C         G          C
Grandeur, Light and Mercy
  F       C                G
Words, Perfection and Names
  C         G          C
Might and Will and Knowledge
  F
Power, Speech, Questions and Honor
  C            G             C
Sovereignty, Dominion and Loftiness
```

Mount your Steeds

by Phil Lucas - *Lift Up Your Voices and Sing*, Vol. 3, CD

VERSE 1

```
                Em         D              Em
Mount your steeds, O heroes of God
      C         D           Em
The Promised Day has come!
 Em              Am        Em    Am
Heed not your weakness or your frailties
 Em                      C   D    Em
Fix your gaze on the Almighty
```

```
                Em         D              Em
Mount your steeds, O heroes of God
      C         D           Em
The Promised Day has come!
   Em           Am        Em         Am
A stream of years have passed us by
 Em                C         D              Em
Since the Blessed Beauty raised His cry
```

```
                Em         D              Em
Mount your steeds, O heroes of God
      C         D           Em
The Promised Day has come!
 Em              Am         Em        Am
The veils of glory have been cast down
 Em                   C         D          Em
The Promised One has come now circle 'round
```

(Verse 1)

One Planet, One People

Unknown Origin

```
 D                                G
We're all living in a dream of one world
                D                           A
Hoping that everyone will, love as they were meant to love
 D                                G
We're all living in a dream of one world
                D                           A
Hoping that everyone will, live as they were meant to live
```

CHORUS
```
G          A
One planet, one people,
D
Please God, we may achieve it
G          A          D
One planet, one people, please
```

```
 D                               G
We're all living in a dream of world peace
               D                         A
Hoping that everyone one sees, a world of love and unity
 D                               G
We're all living in a dream of world peace
                D                           A
A world of different countries, living in peace and harmony
```

(Chorus x2)

One Heart, Ruby Red
by Donna Taylor - *Jeff Jones Live in Concert, CD*

CHORUS

```
 Am          Dm           Am          Dm           Am          Dm
One heart ruby red. One heart ruby red. One heart ruby red
    Am          E7       Am
Beats the heart of man
```

```
 Am                       Dm           Am      Dm
Walking down the street I met a friend
    Am            Dm              Am      Dm
A friend with skin of golden brown
 Am       Dm   Am  Dm   Am         E7                Am
Suffering, suffer-ing-ing, with his head a hanging down
```
(chorus)

```
 Am                       Dm           Am      Dm
Walking down the street I met a friend
    Am            Dm               Am      Dm
A friend with skin of midnight black
 Am       Dm   Am  Dm   Am         E7                Am
Suffering, suffer-ing-ing, with his head a hanging down
```
(chorus)

```
 Am                       Dm           Am      Dm
Walking down the street I met a friend
    Am            Dm             Am   Dm
A friend with skin of snowy white
 Am       Dm   Am  Dm   Am         E7                Am
Suffering, suffer-ing-ing, with his head a hanging down
```
(chorus)

```
 Am                       Dm            Am    Dm
Walking down the street they all did meet
       Am               Dm                  Am         Dm
Three friends with skin of brown and black and white
 Am       Dm  Am  Dm   Am          E7                 Am
Softly, soft-ly -ly, softly they walked into the night
```
(chorus)

```
  Am                    Dm            Am        Dm
When a friend can meet another friend
      Am            Dm           Am         Dm
And when for hate there's love instead
  Am         Dm              Am   Dm Am       E7           Am
'Neath one cloak of varied hue,   beats one heart of ruby red
```
(chorus)

Prince of Peace
Words & Music by Lloyd Haynes - *Lift Up Your Voices*, Vol. 1, CD

CHORUS
```
        Em            D         Em
They call Him the Prince of Peace
              Em          D         Em
They call Him the Prince of Peace
         C         B7       C      B7
From Constantinople to Adrianople
        Am         B7           Em
To Acca, the prison by the sea
```

```
   Em
There lived a Man across the ocean
                   Am              B7
There lived a Man across the sea
                 Em                Em
He spoke of love, He spoke of justice
              Am    B7      Em
He spoke to man of unity
```

(Chorus)

```
   Em
His teachings spread from king to layman
                Am            B7
His teachings spread to all mankind
               Em               Em
His teachings took in all religions
              Am         B7     Em
And left no helpless soul behind
```

(Chorus)

Queen of Carmel

by Jean Murday - *Lift Up Your Voices*, Vol.2, CD

```
   G       C        G  Em      C       D         G
Standing on the mountain, looking across the bay
       G       C       G  Em      C       D        G
The Queen of Carmel reigns, she reigns majestically
```

CHORUS
```
  C   D     G  Em      C    D           G
Cry out, oh Zion!    Cry out to your Lord
  C   D     G  Em     C      D       C       D
Cry out, oh Zion;    circle 'round in adoration
 C       D         G
 Circle 'round your Lord
```

```
    G       C        G       Em       C      D  G
Robed in white and crowned in gold, she stands for unity
    G      C      G    Em       C       D      G
Shining on the Throne of God, she lights the Seeker's way
```

(Chorus)

```
      G        C      G      Em      C    D   G
The Promised One has come to Thee Whose glory we acclaim
   G      C     G    Em      C      D      G
God will sail His ark on thee as written in the Book of Names
```

(Chorus)

```
      G       C      G         Em
Unto God, the Lord of Lords belongs
     C        D       G
 the kingdom of earth and heaven
   G      C    G         Em        C    D    G
Land and sea proclaim this day, the day of revelation
```

(Chorus x2)

See Me Beautiful

Music and lyrics by Red & Kathy Grammer - *Teaching Peace*, CD

      C
See me beautiful
              C7
Look for the best in me
           F
It's what I really am
          F
And all I want to be
     C
It may take some time
    G
May be hard to find
    G
See me beautiful

     C
See me beautiful
       C7
Each and every day
         F
Could you take a chance
        F
Could you find a way
         C
To see me shining through
     G
Everything I do
    G
See me beautiful

Shine Your Light on Me Bahá'u'lláh
Unknown Origin

Shine Your light on me, Baha'u'llah
                C
I am over here, Baha'u'llah
                C
Shine Your light on me, Baha'u'llah
                G7
Glorea, glorea
       C

Shine your light on us Baha'u'llah
                C
We are over here, Baha'u'llah
      C
Shine Your light on us, Baha'u'llah
                G7
Glorea, Glorea
      C

Help us teach Your Cause, Baha'u'llah
                C
Help us love mankind Baha'u'llah
     C
Help us serve mankind Baha'llah
            G7
Glorea Glorea
       C

Singing Wind

By Phyllis Day

      C   **G7**
The wind is singing in the mountains
 G7   **C**
Across the valley and the plains
       C   **F**   **C**   **G7**   **C**
And calling joyous in the islands. Let love and unity reign
    C   **F**   **C**   **C**   **F**   **C**
Let love and unity reign. Let love and unity reign
    C   **F**   **C**   **G7**   **C**
The wind is singing in the mountain. Let love and unity reign

     C   **G7**
The crickets crying in the valley
G7   **C**
Can't see the brilliance of the dawn
    C   **F**   **C**   **G7**   **C**
Can't hear the singing in the mountains. The Promised One is come
   C   **F**   **C**   **C**   **F**   **C**
The Promised One is come. The Promised One is come
    C   **F**   **C**   **G7**   **C**
The wind is singing in the mountain. Let love and unity reign

      C   **G7**
So let us shout it from the mountains
G7   **C**
And fill the world with a new song
    C   **F**   **C**   **G7**   **C**
The wind is singing in the mountains. Bahá'u'lláh has come

C   **F**   **C**   **C**   **F**   **C**
Baha'u'llah has come. Baha'u'llah has come
   C   **F**   **C**   **G7**   **C**
The wind is singing in the mountains. Bahá'u'lláh has come

Tell the Truth
Unknown Origin

VERSE

When you tell the **C** truth (echo)
You win people's **G** trust (echo)
Always tell **G** the truth (echo)
You must, **C** you must

CHORUS

 F
When you tell the truth (echo)
  C
You'll never feel ashamed
G   **C**
God will be pleased with you
 F
If you tell a lie
  C
You surely will be blamed
  D7   **G**
And maybe lose a friend or two

(Verse)

(Chorus)

(Verse)

Teaching Peace

Music & lyrics by Red and Kathy Grammer - *Teaching Peace*, CD

CHORUS

```
   D                A
Teaching peace all the world around
   A                  A7
You and me, every city every town
 D                                        G
One by one, in our work and in our play
  G              D              A           D
We are teaching peace by what we do and what we say
```

```
             A
Its up to us
                D
To show we care
             A                      D
Reaching out to everybody, everywhere
              G
Heart to heart
              D
Friend to friend
             E                                  A
Circling all around the world and back again - (Chorus)
```

```
              A
So take my hand
             D
And come along
              A                                      D
It's time to sing the world a brand new song
                G
So sing it loud
                D
And sing it clear
              E                        A
Altogether now so everyone can hear - (Chorus)
```

That is How Bahá'ís Should Be
Unknown Origin

```
C
I love the Master
        G
The Master loves me
    G           G7              C
He shows me how Bahá'ís should be
   C7           F         Dm
Trusting in God faithfully
   G7                      C
That is how Bahá'ís should be


C
I love the Master
        G
The Master loves me
    G           G7              C
He shows me how Bahá'ís should be
   C7         F          Dm
Praying for guidance constantly
   G7                      C
That is how Bahá'ís should be


C
I love the Master
        G
The Master loves me
    G           G7              C
He shows me how Bahá'ís should be
   C7          F         Dm
God's Will, not my will my prayer will be
   G7                      C
That is how Bahá'ís should be
```

Songs - 75

This Little Light of Mine
Traditional gospel song

CHORUS

  G
This little light of mine, Lord, I'm gonna let it shine
  D   **G**
This little light of mine, Lord, I'm gonna let it shine
  G
This little light of mine, Lord, I'm gonna let it shine
       D   **D7**   **G**
Let it shine, let it shine, let it shine

  G
All over the world now, I'm gonna let it shine
  D   **G**
All over the world now, I'm gonna let it shine
  G
All over the world now, I'm gonna let it shine
       D   **D7**   **G**
Let it shine, let it shine, let it shine

(Chorus)

  G
Put it under a bushel, ..No! I'm gonna let it shine
  D   **G**
Put it under a bushel, ..No! I'm gonna let it shine
  G
Put it under a bushel, ..No! I'm gonna let it shine
       D   **D7**   **G**
Let it shine, let it shine, let it shine

(Chorus)

  G
You can't blow my little light out, I'm gonna let it shine
  D   **G**
You can't blow my little light out, I'm gonna let it shine
  G
You can't blow my little light out, I'm gonna let it shine
       D   **D7**   **G**
Let it shine, let it shine, let it shine

(Chorus)

Toko Zani
Zulu song from Swaziland

```
  G              D7
Toko zani nina laba wanki
   D7           G
Le li langa lakukana
   G              D7
Toko zani nina laba wanki
   D7           G
Le li langa lakukana
    C           G
Toko lako la luku Baha
 D7             G
Um lama wah lampa
   C            G
Kaday kuday si liendole
  D7     G        D7       G
Yá Bahá'u'l-Abhá, ti Yá Bahá'u'l-Abhá
```

```
    G                       D7
Rejoice, rejoice for a new day has dawned
     D7                       G
The whole wide world is all one fold
    G                       D7
Rejoice, rejoice for a new day has dawned
     D7                      G
The plan of God has now been told
       C                  G
The Promised One by the name of Bahá
 D7               G
Came to bring a new day
    C             G
Let us be happy, let us say
  D7     G         D7       G
Yá Bahá'u'l-Abhá, say Yá Bahá'u'l-Abhá
```

Truthfulness
Ruhi Institute

```
    C            G             D          G
Truthfulness is brighter than the light of the sun
    C            G             D          G
Truthfulness is brighter than the light of the sun
         C          G         D          G
With truthfulness, O people, beautify your tongues
         C          G         D          G
With truthfulness, O people, beautify your tongues


   C       G        D        G
Honesty adorns the soul of everyone
   C       G        D        G
Honesty adorns the soul of everyone
   C       G            D          G
Honesty is brighter than the light of the sun
   C       G            D          G
Honesty is brighter than the light of the sun
```

(repeat all)

We are Drops

Hawaiian unity song - Unknown Origin

           C
We are drops (echo)
         C
Of one ocean (echo)
          F
We are waves (echo)
       G
Of one sea (echo)

CHORUS

              C
Come and join us, come and join us
        F
In our quest for unity
        C   **G**   **C**
It's a way of life for you and me

          C   **C**
We are flowers (echo), of one garden (echo)
         F   **G**
We are leaves (echo), of one tree (echo) - **(Chorus)**

         C   **C**
All the earth is (echo), but one country (echo)
     F   **G**
Man is one (echo), can't you see (echo) - **(Chorus)**

        C   **C**
Black and white (echo), red and yellow (echo)
      F   **G**
Lovely colours (echo), for all to see (echo) - **(Chorus)**

        C   **G**   **C**
It's a way of life for you and me

We have Come to Sing Praises

We have Come to Sing Praises, CD
Sung gospel style without guitar

We have come to sing praises to our Lord
We have come to sing praises to our Lord
Allah'u'abha, Ya Baha'ul'abha
We have come to sing praises to our Lord

We have come to give honor to our Lord
We have come to give honor to our Lord
Allah'u'abha, Ya Baha'ul'abha
We have come to give honor to our Lord

We have come to give thanks to our Lord
We have come to give thanks to our Lord
Allah'u'abha, Ya Baha'ul'abha
We have come to give thanks to our Lord

We have come to sing praises to our Lord
We have come to sing praises to our Lord
Allah'u'abha, Ya Baha'ul'abha
We have come to sing praises to our Lord

With Two Wings

Music and lyrics by Red & Kathy Grammer, *Teaching Peace*, CD

CHORUS

```
              C
With two wings, we can soar through the air
              G              C
With two wings, we can go most anywhere
              C              F
With two wings, we can sail through the sky
              C  G           C
With two wings, we can fly - (repeat Chorus)
```

```
              G              C
Males:    I am one wing, father and brother
              G              C
          By myself, all I can do is flutter
              F              C
          I'm only one wing, I need the other
              G              C
          For the Dove of Peace to fly
```

```
              G              C
Females:  I am one wing, sister and mother
              G              C
          By myself all I can do is flutter
              F              C
          I'm only one wing, I need the other
              G              C
          For the Dove of Peace to fly - (Chorus)
```

```
              G
Females:  I am one voice
              C
Males:    I am another
              G
Females:  I'm half of the world
              C
Males:    And I am the other
              F              C
All:      When we learn to work together
              G              C
          Then the Dove of Peace will fly - (Chorus)
```

Would You Give Your Life to Bahá'u'lláh

by Joannie Lincoln - Lift Up Your Voices, Vol. 2, CD

```
                 Am     E7            Am        Am
Would you give your heart - to Baha'u'llah
                 Am     G             E7        E7
Would you give your heart - to Baha'u'llah
              Am      G         Am         E7
Would you be a flame of fire, a river of life
      Am                          E7           Am      Am
Give your heart (give your heart) - to Bahá'u'lláh

              Am    E7           Am     Am
Yes, I'd give my heart - to Baha'u'llah
              Am    G            E7     E7
Yes, I'd give my heart - to Baha'u'llah
        Am       G         Am        E7
I'd be a flame of fire, a river of life
     Am                         E7          Am
Give my heart (give my heart) - to Bahá'u'lláh


                  Am     E7            Am       Am
Would you teach the Cause - of Baha'u'llah
                  Am     G             E7       E7
Would you teach the Cause - of Baha'u'llah
              Am    G              Am           E7
Would you teach your brothers and sisters, your fellow man
        Am                          E7            Am
Teach the Cause (teach the Cause) - of Bahá'u'lláh

              Am    E7              Am     Am
Yes, I'd teach the Cause - of Baha'u'llah
              Am    G               E7     E7
Yes, I'd teach the Cause - of Baha'u'llah
        Am       G         Am         E7
I'd teach my brothers and sisters, my fellow man
        Am                          E7            Am
Teach the Cause (teach the Cause) - of Bahá'u'lláh
```

```
              Am   E7           Am      Am
Would your give your life - for Baha'u'llah
              Am   G            E7      E7
Would your give your life - for Baha'u'llah
            Am   G      Am              E7
Would you give your earthly possessions, your worldly desires
         Am                  E7              Am
Your whole life (your whole life) - for Bahá'u'lláh


         Am   E7           Am      Am
Yes, I'd give my life - for Baha'u'llah
         Am   G            E7      E7
Yes, I'd give my life - for Baha'u'llah
         Am   G      Am           E7
I'd give my earthly possessions, my worldly desires
       Am                E7            Am
My whole life (my whole life) - for Bahá'u'lláh
```

BLANK PAGE

BLANK PAGE

www.ingramcontent.com/pod-product-compliance
Lightning Source LLC
Chambersburg PA
CBHW060457300426
44113CB00016B/2626